The Book of Astronomical Secrets

By Enoch

Copyright © 2019 Lamp of Trismegistus. All rights reserved. No part of this publication may be reproduced or transmitted in any form or by any means, electronic or mechanical, including photocopying, recording, or by any information storage and retrieval system, without permission in writing from Lamp of Trismegistus. Reviewers may quote brief passages.

ISBN: 978-1-63118-443-7

Christian Apocrypha Series

Other Books in this Series and Related Titles

The Testament of Abraham by Abraham (978-1-63118-441-3)

Book of Dreams by Enoch (978-1-63118-437-6)

Psalms of Solomon by King Solomon (978-1-63118-439-0)

The Lives of Adam and Eve by Moses (978-1-63118-414-7)

The First and Second Gospels of the Infancy of Jesus Christ by Thomas and James (978-1-63118-415-4)

Lost Chapters of the Book of Daniel and Related Writings by Daniel (978-1-63118-417-8)

The Testament of Moses by Moses (978-1-63118-440-6)

The Book of the Watchers by Enoch (978-1-63118-416-1)

The Book of Parables by Enoch (978-1-63118-429-1)

Masonic Symbolism of Easter and the Christ in Masonry by various authors (978-1-63118-434-5)

A Few Masonic Sermons by A. C. Ward & Bascom B. Clarke (978-1-63118-435-2)

Masonic Symbolism of King Solomon's Temple by Albert G. Mackey & others (978-1-63118-442-0)

Cloud Upon the Sanctuary by A. E. Waite & K. Eckartshausen (978-1-63118-438-3)

The Two Great Pillars of Boaz and Jachin by Albert G. Mackey & others (978-1-63118-433-8)

Audio Versions are also Available on Audible and iTunes

Table of Contents

Introduction…7

Prologue…9

Part I:
The Sun…15

Part II:
The Moon and its Phases…21

Part III:
The Lunar Year…23

Part IV:
The Twelve Windows and Their Portals…27

Part V:
The Four Quarters of the World,
The Seven Mountains, Seven Rivers
and Seven Great Islands…29

Part VI:
*The Sun and Moon;
The Waxing and Waning of the Moon*…31

Part VII:
Recapitulation of Several of the Laws…35

Part VIII:
*Perversion of Nature and the Heavenly Bodies
Due to the Sin of Man*…37

Part XIX:
The Heavenly Tablets and the Mission of Enoch...39

Part X:
The Charge Given to Enoch,
the Four Intercalary Days
and the Stars Which Lead the Seasons
and the Months...41

Introduction

The Apocrypha are a loosely knit series of books, written by early vanguards of Christianity (covering the eras of both the old and new testaments), and which comprise somewhere between about a dozen to several hundred titles, depending on whom you ask and how that person defines "Apocrypha." A small selection of these can still be found included in the Catholic bible, while a majority of the books in question, were abandoned by church officials in the early centuries of Christianity. Many of these apocryphal books were originally considered canon by early followers of Christ, in the first four centuries following his birth. It wasn't until the meeting of the Council of Nicaea in 325, that Emperor Constantine and a group of roughly 300 church bishops, gathered together with the goal of defining, standardizing and unifying an otherwise splintering Christianity, that many of these writings ceased to be included in the newly established canon. Enjoy then, this book as an example, of just one of the many books of the Christian Apocrypha, and be sure to check out other titles in this series.

Prologue

Who is Enoch and why is he so important?

Jude 1:14 describes Enoch as being the seventh generation of man from Adam, while also making reference to Enoch's ability to prophesize. Enoch was born on Seth's side of Adam and Eve's lineage and was the great grandfather of Noah. References to him in the Bible are sparse, but he is most well-known for not having died but instead for having walked away with God. In some Christian and Jewish traditions Enoch is also considered to be a scribe and to have been ordained as a priest by Adam.

Perhaps because of Enoch's unique departure from Earth into heaven, there was a rich tradition of exploring what Enoch's life was like, upon leaving Earth. The events of his time in heaven were often explored in classic rabbinical literature as well as the three primary apocryphal books with his name attached to them. Some modern churches continue to embrace Enoch's importance, including the Ethiopian Orthodox Church and perhaps more notably, the Latter Day Saints.

The full text of the magnum opus commonly known as *The Book of Enoch* or *1 Enoch*, is in fact a collection of five separate and unrelated, apocryphal books, the authorship of which spanned several centuries in history, while the real commonality of all being that they each involve Enoch.

The section which is usually presented as chapters 72 through 82 of *The Book of Enoch* was originally known as the *Book of Astronomical Secrets*, or sometimes it was translated as the *Book of the Courses of the Heavenly Luminaries*. It is most likely the oldest of the five collected texts which comprise the *Book of Enoch*, dating between the third and second centuries B.C. This particular translation comes to us from notable scholar of apocryphal literature, R. H. Charles, who published it in 1917.

Among other things, the book describes an ancient calendar which unsurprisingly has come to be known as the Enoch Calendar. This ancient Enoch Calendar, while it may seem similar on the surface, differs from our modern Gregorian calendar in a significant and affecting way. Most notably, it is a day short. By sacrificing one day a year, the Enoch Calendar was able to present itself in a much more balanced and aesthetic format of 364 days, with four perfectly balanced, equal seasons, all of which consist of three, thirty-day months, followed by a single floating day, each season. The four floating days of the year, one per season, were each given a name, rather than a number. The result of this layout is a 364-day year, in which every calendar day always occurs on the same day of the week, every year.

One scholar of the history of calendars, John Pratt, points out that with only 364 days, the Enoch Calendar would quickly become out of sync with the seasons. So, in only 25 years the seasons would arrive an entire month early. To combat this, Pratt suggests that by adding an extra week at the end of every seventh year (or Sabbatical year), and then adding two extra weeks to every fourth Sabbatical year (or every 28 years), the calendar would essentially be as accurate as the Julian calendar, which was the immediate precursor to the Gregorian calendar, differing in length of the year by only 0.002%.

In this calendar arrangement, Uriel explains to Enoch that the different parts of the year are watched over by different angelic beings, in a hierarchical format. So, there is an angel who rules over each of the 4 seasons, but there are also 12 lesser angels who rule over each of the 12 months, and so on and so forth.

Compared to other entries in the collective Books of Enoch, there is much less in the way of oracles and foretelling; however, there is a bit. That which is presented is much subtler, with Uriel implying to Enoch that the power behind the movement of the stars is strong enough to mislead man into committing wrong deeds.

Throughout the descriptions given by the angel Uriel, there is a lot of talk of "portals" (meaning "gateway"), and the easiest way to understand what Uriel is trying to describe to Enoch, might be to view them as "beginnings." Let's take September, the ninth month of the year, as an example. So, rather than saying, as you or I might, that "at the beginning of September the days continue to become shorter and the nights continue to become longer," the angel instead, poetically describes the sun as entering into the ninth portal.

In addition to portals, there are also frequent references to numbers. These are usually pretty easy to account for, but it's also important to keep in mind that the same number may sometimes be applied in more than one manner. As well, sometimes the numbers are symbolic and consequently less straight-forward and thus, somewhat more philosophical in nature.

The number twelve is most likely always in reference to the twelve months of the year or similarly the twelve zodiacal signs, which themselves represent the solar year separated into twelve parts. By the same account, references to the number six in this text, are likely referencing half of one solar year.

The number four is sometimes going to be referring to the four seasons of the year, while at other times it's going to be referring to the four cardinal directions of North, South, East and West. By doing that, what is really being referred to is the concept that the seasons of the year themselves, can immediately change, depending on what part of the globe you may be standing on. Summer in the northern hemisphere is Winter in the southern hemisphere and so forth. The number four may also, at times, have subtle, underlying allusions to the four classical elements of Earth, Water, Fire and Air, which were of great importance to the ancients.

Slightly more complicated is the number seven, within the context of this book. Typically, in texts from this era, references to the number seven would be allusions to the seven classical planets, each of which have certain philosophical attributes attached to them. However, regarding some of the instances of usage in this case which center around the discussion of the moon, I believe that the number seven is being used as a rough representation of one fourth of a lunar month. In murkier instance, such as references to the seven mountains, rivers or islands, these are most certainly allusions, as previously stated, to the seven classical planets.

Of course, throughout all of this, it's also important to remain mindful and keep from over-analyzing the numbers themselves, and remember, as Freud has been accused of saying, that sometimes a cigar is just a cigar. Or, in this instance, sometimes a number is just doing its job as a number and isn't concealing any deeper philosophical meaning.

Enjoy then, this book before you and the astronomical knowledge contained therein, as it was given to Enoch by the archangel Uriel, during Enoch's trips through Heaven. In addition to the calendar itself, Uriel bestows upon Enoch information relating to laws by which the sun, moon, stars and winds are governed as well as other mysteries of the Universe.

Part I

The Sun

The book of the courses of the luminaries of the heaven, the relations of each, according to their classes, their dominion and their seasons, according to their names and places of origin, and according to their months, which Uriel, the holy angel, who was with me, who is their guide, showed me; and he showed me all their laws exactly as they are, and how it is with regard to all the years of the world and unto eternity, till the new creation is accomplished which endureth till eternity.

And this is the first law of the luminaries: the luminary, the Sun, has its rising in the eastern portals of the heaven, and its setting in the western portals of the heaven.

And I saw six portals in which the sun rises, and six portals in which the sun sets and the moon rises and sets in these portals, and the leaders of the stars and those whom they lead: six in the east and six in the west, and all following each other in accurately corresponding order: also many windows to the right and left of these portals.

And first there goes forth the great luminary, named the Sun, and his circumference is like the circumference of the heaven, and he is quite filled with illuminating and heating fire.

The chariot on which he ascends, the wind drives, and the sun goes down from the heaven and returns through the north in order to reach the east, and is so guided that he comes to the appropriate portal and shines in the face of the heaven.

In this way he rises in the first month in the great portal, which is the fourth of six portals in the east.

And in that fourth portal from which the sun rises in the first month are twelve window-openings, from which proceed a flame when they are opened in their season.

When the sun rises in the heaven, he comes forth through that fourth portal thirty mornings in succession, and sets accurately in the fourth portal in the west of the heaven.

And during this period the day becomes daily longer and the night nightly shorter to the thirtieth morning.

On that day the day is longer than the night by a ninth part, and the day amounts exactly to ten parts and the night to eight parts.

And the sun rises from that fourth portal, and sets in the fourth and returns to the fifth portal of the east thirty mornings, and rises from it and sets in the fifth portal.

And then the day becomes longer by two parts and amounts to eleven parts, and the night becomes shorter and amounts to seven parts.

And it returns to the east and enters into the sixth portal, and rises and sets in the sixth portal one-and-thirty mornings on account of its sign.

On that day the day becomes longer than the night, and the day becomes double the night, and the day becomes twelve parts, and the night is shortened and becomes six parts.

And the sun mounts up to make the day shorter and the night longer, and the sun returns to the east and enters into the sixth portal, and rises from it and sets thirty mornings.

And when thirty mornings are accomplished, the day decreases by exactly one part, and becomes eleven parts, and the night seven.

And the sun goes forth from that sixth portal in the west, and goes to the east and rises in the fifth portal for thirty mornings, and sets in the west again in the fifth western portal.

On that day the day decreases by two parts, and amounts to ten parts and the night to eight parts.

And the sun goes forth from that fifth portal and sets in the fifth portal of the west, and rises in the fourth portal for one-and-thirty mornings on account of its sign, and sets in the west.

On that day the day is equalized with the night, and becomes of equal length, and the night amounts to nine parts and the day to nine parts.

And the sun rises from that portal and sets in the west, and returns to the east and rises thirty mornings in the third portal and sets in the west in the third portal.

And on that day the night becomes longer than the day, and night becomes longer than night, and day shorter than day till the thirtieth morning, and the night amounts exactly to ten parts and the day to eight parts.

And the sun rises from that third portal and sets in the third portal in the west and returns to the east, and for thirty mornings rises in the second portal in the east, and in like manner sets in the second portal in the west of the heaven.

And on that day the night amounts to eleven parts and the day to seven parts.

And the sun rises on that day from that second portal and sets in the west in the second portal, and returns to the east into the first portal for one-and-thirty mornings, and sets in the first portal in the west of the heaven.

And on that day the night becomes longer and amounts to the double of the day: and the night amounts exactly to twelve parts and the day to six.

And the sun has therewith traversed the divisions of his orbit and turns again on those divisions of his orbit, and enters that portal thirty mornings and sets also in the west opposite to it.

And on that night has the night decreased in length by a ninth part, and the night has become eleven parts and the day seven parts.

And the sun has returned and entered into the second portal in the east, and returns on those his divisions of his orbit for thirty mornings, rising and setting.

And on that day the night decreases in length, and the night amounts to ten parts and the day to eight.

And on that day the sun rises from that portal, and sets in the west, and returns to the east, and rises in the third portal for one-and-thirty mornings, and sets in the west of the heaven.

On that day the night decreases and amounts to nine parts, and the day to nine parts, and the night is equal to the day and the year is exactly as to its days three hundred and sixty-four.

And the length of the day and of the night, and the shortness of the day and of the night arise--through the course of the sun these distinctions are made.

So, it comes that its course becomes daily longer, and its course nightly shorter.

And this is the law and the course of the sun, and his return as often as he returns sixty times and rises, *i.e.* the great luminary which is named the Sun, for ever and ever.

And that which thus rises is the great luminary, and is so

named according to its appearance, according as the Lord commanded.

As he rises, so he sets and decreases not, and rests not, but runs day and night, and his light is sevenfold brighter than that of the moon; but as regards size they are both equal.

Part II

The Moon and its Phases

And after this law I saw another law dealing with the smaller luminary, which is named the Moon.

And her circumference is like the circumference of the heaven, and her chariot in which she rides is driven by the wind, and light is given to her in definite measure.

And her rising and setting change every month: and her days are like the days of the sun, and when her light is uniform (*i.e.* full) it amounts to the seventh part of the light of the sun.

And thus, she rises. And her first phase in the east comes forth on the thirtieth morning: and on that day she becomes visible, and constitutes for you the first phase of the moon on the thirtieth day together with the sun in the portal where the sun rises.

And the one half of her goes forth by a seventh part, and her whole circumference is empty, without light, with the exception of one-seventh part of it, and the fourteenth part of her light.

And when she receives one-seventh part of the half of her light, her light amounts to one-seventh part and the half thereof.

And she sets with the sun, and when the sun rises the moon rises with him and receives the half of one part of light, and in that night at the beginning of her morning, in the commencement of the lunar day, the moon sets with the sun, and is invisible that night, with the fourteen parts and the half of one of them.

And she rises on that day with exactly a seventh part, and comes forth and recedes from the rising of the sun, and in her remaining days she becomes bright in the remaining thirteen parts.

Part III

The Lunar Year

And I saw another course, a law for her, and how according to that law she performs her monthly revolution.

And all these Uriel, the holy angel who is the leader of them all, showed to me, and their positions, and I wrote down their positions as he showed them to me, and I wrote down their months as they were, and the appearance of their lights till fifteen days were accomplished.

In single seventh parts she accomplishes all her light in the east, and in single seventh parts accomplishes all her darkness in the west.

And in certain months she alters her settings, and in certain months she pursues her own peculiar course.

In two months, the moon sets with the sun: in those two middle portals the third and the fourth.

She goes forth for seven days, and turns about and returns again through the portal where the sun rises, and accomplishes all her light: and she recedes from the sun, and in eight days enters the sixth portal from which the sun goes forth.

And when the sun goes forth from the fourth portal she goes forth seven days, until she goes forth from the fifth and turns back again in seven days into the fourth portal and accomplishes all her light: and she recedes and enters into the first portal in eight days.

And she returns again in seven days into the fourth portal from which the sun goes forth.

Thus, I saw their position--how the moons rose and the sun set in those days.

And if five years are added together the sun has an overplus of thirty days, and all the days which accrue to it for one of those five years, when they are full, amount to 364 days.

And the overplus of the sun and of the stars amounts to six days: in 5 years 6 days every year come to 30 days: and the moon falls behind the sun and stars to the number of 30 days.

And the sun and the stars bring in all the years exactly, so that they do not advance or delay their position by a single day unto eternity; but complete the years with perfect justice in 364 days.

In 3 years, there are 1092 days, and in 5 years 1820 days, so that in 8 years there are 2912 days.

For the moon alone, the days amount in 3 years to 1062 days, and in 5 years she falls 50 days behind.

And in 5 years there are 1770 days, so that for the moon the days in 8 years amount to 2832 days.

For in 8 years she falls behind to the amount of 80 days; all the days she falls behind in 8 years are 80.

And the year is accurately completed in conformity with their world-stations and the stations of the sun, which rise from the portals through which it, the sun, rises and sets 30 days.

And the leaders of the heads of the thousands, who are placed over the whole creation and over all the stars, have also to do with the four intercalary days, being inseparable from their office, according to the reckoning of the year, and these render service on the four days which are not reckoned in the reckoning of the year.

And owing to them men go wrong therein, for those luminaries truly render service on the world-stations, one in the first portal, one in the third portal of the heaven, one in the fourth portal, and one in the sixth portal, and the exactness of the year is accomplished through its separate three hundred and sixty-four stations.

For the signs and the times and the years and the days the angel Uriel showed to me, whom the Lord of glory hath set for ever over all the luminaries of the heaven, in the heaven and in the world, that they should rule on the face of the heaven and be seen on the earth, and be leaders for the day and the night, *i.e.* the sun, moon, and stars, and all the ministering creatures which make their revolution in all the chariots of the heaven.

In like manner twelve doors Uriel showed me, open in the circumference of the sun's chariot in the heaven, through which the rays of the sun break forth: and from them is warmth diffused over the earth, when they are opened at their appointed seasons.

And for the winds and the spirit of the dew when they are opened, standing open in the heavens at the ends.

As for the twelve portals in the heaven, at the ends of the earth, out of which go forth the sun, moon, and stars, and all the works of heaven in the east and in the west.

There are many windows open to the left and right of them, and one window at its appointed season produces warmth, corresponding, as these do, to those doors from which the stars come forth according as He has commanded them, and wherein they set corresponding to their number.

And I saw chariots in the heaven, running in the world, above those portals in which revolve the stars that never set.

And one is larger than all the rest, and it is that that makes its course through the entire world.

Part IV

The Twelve Windows and Their Portals

And at the ends of the earth I saw twelve portals open to all the quarters of the heaven, from which the winds go forth and blow over the earth.

Three of them are open on the face (*i.e.* the east) of the heavens, and three in the west, and three on the south of the heaven, and three on the north.

Through four of these come winds of blessing and prosperity, and from the other eight come hurtful winds: when they are sent, they bring destruction on all the earth and on the water upon it, and on all who dwell thereon, and on everything which is in the water and on the land.

And the first wind from those portals, called the east wind, comes forth through the first portal which is in the east, inclining towards the south: from it come forth desolation, drought, heat, and destruction. And through the second portal in the middle comes what is fitting, and from it there come rain and fruitfulness and prosperity and dew; and through the third portal which lies toward the north come cold and drought.

And after these are the south winds, through three portals: through the first portal of them inclining to the east comes forth a hot wind. And through the middle portal next to it there come forth fragrant smells, and dew and rain, and prosperity and health. And through the third portal lying to the west come forth dew and rain, locusts and desolation.

And after these are the north winds: from the seventh portal in the east come dew and rain, locusts and desolation. And from the middle portal come in a direct direction health and rain and dew and prosperity; and through the third portal in the west come cloud and hoar-frost, and snow and rain, and dew and locusts.

And after these are the west winds: through the first portal adjoining the north come forth dew and hoar-frost, and cold and snow and frost. And from the middle portal come forth dew and rain, and prosperity and blessing; and through the last portal which adjoins the south come forth drought and desolation, and burning and destruction.

And the twelve portals of the four quarters of the heaven are therewith completed, and all their laws and all their plagues and all their benefactions have I shown to thee, my son Methuselah.

Part V

The Four Quarters of the World: The Seven Mountains, Seven Rivers and Seven Great Islands

And the first quarter is called the east, because it is the first: and the second, the south, because the Most High will descend there, yea, there in quite a special sense will He who is blessed for ever descend.

And the west quarter is named the diminished, because there all the luminaries of the heaven wane and go down.

And the fourth quarter, named the north, is divided into three parts: the first of them is for the dwelling of men: and the second contains seas of water, and the abysses and forests and rivers, and darkness and clouds; and the third part contains the garden of righteousness.

I saw seven high mountains, higher than all the mountains which are on the earth: and thence comes forth hoar-frost, and days, seasons, and years pass away.

I saw seven rivers on the earth larger than all the rivers: one of them coming from the west pours its waters into the Great Sea.

And these two come from the north to the sea and pour their waters into the Erythraean Sea in the east.

And the remaining four come forth on the side of the north to their own sea, two of them to the Erythraean Sea, and two into the Great Sea and discharge themselves there and some say: into the desert.

Seven great islands I saw in the sea and in the mainland: two in the mainland and five in the Great Sea.

Part VI

The Sun and Moon: The Waxing and Waning of the Moon

And the names of the sun are the following: the first Orjares, and the second Tomas.

And the moon has four names: the first name is Asonja, the second Ebla, the third Benase, and the fourth Erae.

These are the two great luminaries: their circumference is like the circumference of the heaven, and the size of the circumference of both is alike.

In the circumference of the sun there are seven portions of light which are added to it more than to the moon, and in definite measures it is s transferred till the seventh portion of the sun is exhausted.

And they set and enter the portals of the west, and make their revolution by the north, and come forth through the eastern portals on the face of the heaven.

And when the moon rises one-fourteenth part appears in the heaven: the light becomes full in her: on the fourteenth day she accomplishes her light.

And fifteen parts of light are transferred to her till the fifteenth day, when her light is accomplished, according to the sign of the year, and she becomes fifteen parts, and the moon grows by the addition of fourteenth parts.

And in her waning, the moon decreases on the first day to fourteen parts of her light, on the second to thirteen parts of light, on the third to twelve, on the fourth to eleven, on the fifth to ten, on the sixth to nine, on the seventh to eight, on the eighth to seven, on the ninth to six, on the tenth to five, on the eleventh to four, on the twelfth to three, on the thirteenth to two, on the fourteenth to the half of a seventh, and all her remaining light disappears wholly on the fifteenth.

And in certain months the month has twenty-nine days and once twenty-eight.

And Uriel showed me another law: when light is transferred to the moon, and on which side it is transferred to her by the sun.

During all the period during which the moon is growing in her light, she is transferring it to herself when opposite to the sun during fourteen days her light is accomplished in the heaven, and when she is illumined throughout, her light is accomplished full in the heaven.

And on the first day she is called the new moon, for on that day the light rises upon her.

She becomes full moon exactly on the day when the sun

sets in the west, and from the east she rises at night, and the moon shines the whole night through till the sun rises over against her and the moon is seen over against the sun.

On the side, whence the light of the moon comes forth, there again she wanes till all the light vanishes and all the days of the month are at an end, and her circumference is empty, void of light.

And three months she makes of thirty days, and at her time she makes three months of twenty-nine days each, in which she accomplishes her waning in the first period of time, and in the first portal for one hundred and seventy-seven days.

And in the time of her going out she appears for three months of thirty days each, and for three months she appears of twenty-nine each.

At night she appears like a man for twenty days each time, and by day she appears like the heaven, and there is nothing else in her save her light.

Part VII

Recapitulation of Several of the Laws

And now, my son, I have shown thee everything, and the law of all the stars of the heaven is completed.

And he showed me all the laws of these for every day, and for every season of bearing rule, and for every year, and for its going forth, and for the order prescribed to it every month and every week:

And the waning of the moon which takes place in the sixth portal: for in this sixth portal her light is accomplished, and after that there is the beginning of the waning:

And the waning which takes place in the first portal in its season, till one hundred and seventy-seven days are accomplished, reckoned according to weeks: twenty-five weeks and two days.

She falls behind the sun and the order of the stars exactly five days in the course of one period, and when this place which thou seest has been traversed.

Such is the picture and sketch of every luminary which Uriel the archangel, who is their leader, showed unto me.

Part VIII

Perversion of Nature and the Heavenly Bodies Due to the Sin of Men

And in those days the angel Uriel answered and said to me:

"Behold, I have shown thee everything, Enoch, and I have revealed everything to thee that thou shouldst see this sun and this moon, and the leaders of the stars of the heaven and all those who turn them, their tasks and times and departures.

"And in the days of the sinners the years shall be shortened, And their seed shall be tardy on their lands and fields, And all things on the earth shall alter, And shall not appear in their time, And the rain shall be kept back, And the heaven shall withhold it.

"And in those times the fruits of the earth shall be backward, And shall not grow in their time, And the fruits of the trees shall be withheld in their time.

"And the moon shall alter her order, And not appear at her time.

"And in those days the sun shall be seen and he shall journey in the evening on the extremity of the great chariot in the west, And shall shine more brightly than accords with the order of light.

"And many chiefs of the stars shall transgress the prescribed order, And these shall alter their orbits and tasks, And not appear at the seasons prescribed to them.

"And the whole order of the stars shall be concealed from the sinners, And the thoughts of those on the earth shall err concerning them, And they shall be altered from all their ways, Yea, they shall err and take them to be gods.

"And evil shall be multiplied upon them, And punishment shall come upon them So as to destroy all."

Part IX

The Heavenly Tablets and the Mission of Enoch

And Uriel said unto me, "Observe, Enoch, these heavenly tablets, And read what is written thereon, And mark every individual fact."

And I observed the heavenly tablets, and read everything which was written thereon and understood everything, and read the book of all the deeds of mankind, and of all the children of flesh that shall be upon the earth to the remotest generations.

And forthwith I blessed the great Lord the King of glory for ever, in that He has made all the works of the world, And I extolled the Lord because of His patience, And blessed Him because of the children of men.

And after that I said, "Blessed is the man who dies in righteousness and goodness, Concerning whom, there is no book of unrighteousness written, And against whom no day of judgement shall be found."

And those seven holy ones brought me and placed me on the earth before the door of my house, and said to me, "Declare everything to thy son Methuselah, and show to all thy children that no flesh is righteous in the sight of the Lord, for He is their Creator.

"One year we will leave thee with thy son, till thou givest thy last commands, that thou mayest teach thy children and record it for them, and testify to all thy children; and in the second year they shall take thee from their midst.

"Let thy heart be strong, For the good shall announce righteousness to the good; The righteous with the righteous shall rejoice, And shall offer congratulation to one another.

"But the sinners shall die with the sinners, And the apostate go down with the apostate.

"And those who practice righteousness shall die on account of the deeds of men, And be taken away on account of the doings of the godless."

And in those days, they ceased to speak to me, and I came to my people, blessing the Lord of the world.

Part X

The Charge Given to Enoch, the Four Intercalary Days and the Stars Which Lead the Seasons and the Months

And now, my son Methuselah, all these things I am recounting to thee and writing down for thee, and I have revealed to thee everything, and given thee books concerning all these: so preserve, my son Methuselah, the books from thy father's hand, and see that thou deliver them to the generations of the world.

I have given Wisdom to thee and to thy children, And thy children that shall be to thee, That they may give it to their children for generations, Namely this wisdom that passeth their thought.

And those who understand it shall not sleep, But shall listen with the ear that they may learn this wisdom, And it shall please those that eat thereof better than good food.

Blessed are all the righteous, blessed are all those who walk in the way of righteousness and sin not as the sinners, in the reckoning of all their days in which the sun traverses the heaven, entering into and departing from the portals for thirty days with the heads of thousands of the order of the stars, together with the four which are intercalated which divide the four portions of the year, which lead them and enter with them four days.

Owing to them men shall be at fault and not reckon them in the whole reckoning of the year: yea, men shall be at fault, and not recognize them accurately.

For they belong to the reckoning of the year and are truly recorded thereon forever, one in the first portal and one in the third, and one in the fourth and one in the sixth, and the year is completed in three hundred and sixty-four days.

And the account thereof is accurate and the recorded reckoning thereof exact; for the luminaries, and months and festivals, and years and days, has Uriel shown and revealed to me, to whom the Lord of the whole creation of the world hath subjected the host of heaven.

And he has power over night and day in the heaven to cause the light to give light to men--sun, moon, and stars, and all the powers of the heaven which revolve in their circular chariots.

And these are the orders of the stars, which set in their places, and in their seasons and festivals and months.

And these are the names of those who lead them, who watch that they enter at their times, in their orders, in their seasons, in their months, in their periods of dominion, and in their positions.

Their four leaders who divide the four parts of the year enter first; and after them the twelve leaders of the orders who divide the months; and for the three hundred and sixty days there are heads over thousands who divide the days; and for the four intercalary days there are the leaders which sunder the four parts of the year.

And these heads over thousands are intercalated between leader and leader, each behind a station, but their leaders make the division. And these are the names of the leaders who divide the four parts of the year which are ordained: Milki'el, Hel'emmelek, and Mel'ejal, and Narel.

And the names of those who lead them: Adnar'el, and Ijasusa'el, and Elome'el--these three follow the leaders of the orders, and there is one that follows the three leaders of the orders which follow those leaders of stations that divide the four parts of the year.

In the beginning of the year Melkejal rises first and rules, who is named Tam'aini and sun, and all the days of his dominion whilst he bears rule are ninety-one days.

And these are the signs of the days which are to be seen on earth in the days of his dominion: sweat, and heat, and calms; and all the trees bear fruit, and leaves are produced on all the trees, and the harvest of wheat, and the rose-flowers, and all the flowers which come forth in the field, but the trees of the winter season become withered.

And these are the names of the leaders which are under

them: Berka'el, Zelebs'el, and another who is added a head of a thousand, called Hilujaseph: and the days of the dominion of this leader are at an end.

The next leader after him is Hel'emmelek, whom one names the shining sun, and all the days of his light are ninety-one days.

And these are the signs of his days on the earth: glowing heat and dryness, and the trees ripen their fruits and produce all their fruits ripe and ready, and the sheep pair and become pregnant, and all the fruits of the earth are gathered in, and everything that is in the fields, and the winepress: these things take place in the days of his dominion.

These are the names, and the orders, and the leaders of those heads of thousands: Gida'ijal, Ke'el, and He'el, and the name of the head of a thousand which is added to them, Asfa'el': and the days of his dominion are at an end.

www.ingramcontent.com/pod-product-compliance
Lightning Source LLC
LaVergne TN
LVHW041502070426
835507LV00009B/751